D1104202

DESIGN FOR FLOWER EMBROIDERY

Embroidered Furze
From a free drawing in waterproof inks. The embroidery is in silk threads on ivory glazed cotton, and worked in back-stitch, flat-stitch, chain, split-stitch and French knots.

Design by HELEN STREVENS, embroidered interpretation by the AUTHOR.

(*By courtesy of the Needlework Development Scheme*)

TT
773
G4

DESIGN FOR
FLOWER
EMBROIDERY

ELISABETH GEDDES

MILLS & BOON LIMITED

50 GRAFTON WAY LONDON W1

119103

© Elisabeth Geddes 1961

MADE AND PRINTED IN GREAT BRITAIN
BY JARROLD AND SONS LTD, NORWICH

To

I.M.H.

Contents

Acknowledgements

My most sincere thanks to the Needlework Development Scheme, Glasgow, for permitting the use of so many of their photographs in this book. To Margaret F. S. Millar for her invaluable assistance, Messrs. R. Finlayson and J. Gardner for technical advice and help, and Iris Hills for making available numerous reference works from her personal library.

Also to the following publishing companies for kindly allowing me to use material: Messrs. Constable & Co. Ltd and Mr Arthur Waley for permission to use the quotation from *170 Chinese Poems* in the Introduction. Messrs. Penguin Books Ltd for permission to use an adaptation of an original lithograph by Clarke Hutton from *Popular English Art* in the King Penguin Series, in Section One. Messrs. Bernard Quaritch Ltd for permission to use the figures from *Decorative Patterns of the Ancient World* by Sir Flinders Petrie, in Section One, pages 18–22, 24, 26–28. The Clarendon Press, Oxford, for permission to use the quotation in Section Two from *Traditional Methods of Pattern Designing* by A. H. Christie, 1929. Messrs. Chapman & Hall Ltd for permission to use the quotation from *The Craftsman's Plant Book* by Richard Hatton at the beginning of Section Three. Messrs. B. T. Batsford Ltd for permission to use the quotation in Section Four from *Samplers and Stitches* by Mrs Archibald Christie.

Lastly, my thanks to Helen Strevens for allowing me to adapt twelve of her original designs for inclusion in the text.

E. G.

List of Plates

Introduction

My new wife is clever at embroidering silk;
My old wife was good at plain sewing.
Of silk embroidery one can do an inch a day;
Of plain sewing, more than five feet.
Putting her silks by the side of your sewing,
I see that the new will not compare with the old.

(Anon. Chinese first century B.C. from *170 Chinese Poems*
translated by Arthur Waley

PLANTS and flowers are among the most delightful and beautiful of all created things, and, throughout the history of art, have provided designers with a prolific and valuable source of reference. It is beyond doubt that they possess qualities which can be admirably expressed through the medium of embroidery, and indeed, as we know, there were periods in the past when embroidered floral ornament attained great distinction. The purpose of this book, however, is not specifically to trace the historical development of floral needlework, but to attempt to isolate and examine it as a single, though very important, aspect of the craft as a whole.

The position of embroidery today, in relation to its fellow crafts, cannot be said to be altogether happy. There appear to be certain misconceptions regarding its proper function as a decorative art, which are the cause of much bad design in general. There is nothing esoteric about embroidery; it is one of a number of crafts whose concern is with ornament, and the principles of ornamental design apply to it in the same way as they do elsewhere. The lingering tendency to invest it with an exaggerated aura of femininity, which originated in the eighteenth century, has had the unfortunate result of rather isolating it from other creative arts, to its disadvantage.

The history of embroidery in this country has generally been one of separation between designer and worker. The idea that satisfactory work can *only* be produced where designer and executant are one and the same is comparatively recent, and erroneous. An appraisal of past embroidery should be sufficient to prove that during all the best periods there was always a division of labour. The ability to draw and design is given to fewer than is the ability to develop manual skill, and most historic embroidery was produced by workers who had to rely on someone else for their designs. This is also true today, but the difference between now and then is that these earlier designers were skilled artists, their designs reflected sincerely the idiom of their own times and showed an understanding of the medium by which they were expressed. These fundamental requirements are not understood by present-day trade embroidery firms, and the result is the trivial and anachronistic rubbish offered to the modern worker who needs to purchase prepared designs. The sad

13

thing is that no art can survive indefinitely in such a state of inanition but must ultimately wither and die.

Present-day embroidery design would seem to lean towards either of two extremes: one antiquarian and preoccupied with technique, the other superficial and self-consciously "modern". The first approach is characterised by total immunity to the influences of contemporary artistic thought, the second by an attempt to express fashionable ideas of the moment "freely", that is unhindered by consideration of technique. This second approach, where it is sincere, is at least a conscious reaction against the first, and in its less extreme form often produces designs that are both fresh and forward-looking, but it is also vitally necessary to have between these two extremes a large, discriminating and self-critical centre group, if the craft is to stay healthy.

If it is true to say that all art is a commentary on the times which produce it, and is itself governed by sociological trends, how are we to judge the sheer inappropriateness of so much embroidery design today? What are we to make of the hideous "stamped" goods on the market, so trite and irrelevant, in comparison with the charming modern printed textile and wallpaper designs offered on the other hand? It seems completely illogical that such a difference in standard is accepted. Is it the manufacturers or the public who are to blame? Is there really an overwhelming demand for "Jacobean" design, weakly imitating a style integral with the domestic interiors of over three hundred years ago? And why perpetuate the decorative themes of the nineties and earlier periods when embroidery had sunk to its lowest ebb? Is it true that we are so unappreciative of the vitality and invention in current decorative art that we prefer this sort of stuff? Of course it is impossible to approach design with absolute detachment, for our ideas of what is beautiful are bound to be influenced by what public opinion in the past accepted as beautiful, and to this extent we must always be linked with historical tradition, but to continue glorifying the past and ignoring the present is to achieve ultimate stagnation.

It is instinctive in people to wish to use their hands creatively, and there must be many who have limited drawing ability and yet whose urge for self-expression requires something more satisfactory than the performance of mechanical exercises in dictated stitchery. These people are likely to find better subjects for their needle by using contemporary textile design or even studying modern posters where these are flat and decorative, rather than in the banalities of current magazine embroidery "supplements" and trade transfers.

The scope for embroidery today has certainly diminished. It has, for instance, narrowed in its application to dress, excepting religious and ceremonial dress, although there is still a vogue for machine embroidery of a slight nature on lingerie and children's wear, and, according to the whims of *couture*, decoration such as tambour beading, etc., on evening dress and accessories. But in the domestic sphere there are great opportunities, both in the decoration of furnishings for the home, as architectural ornament, i.e. wall-panels and finger-plates, and on personal articles. But it is extremely desirable that we should express our own times in the designs we choose, and the way in which we work them out. The machine, and not the hand craftsman, is our principal producer today, and it is this factor which gives our contemporary life its particular flavour. Just as the old hand methods produced their distinctive styles, so machine manufacture produces its own characteristic shapes and outlines. Embroidered decoration now has to be allied with machine-made doors, windows, chairs and tables, often in houses built from machine-made units, but the severe lines of modern furniture show off quite admirably the rich textural quality of embroidery. In this medium floral motifs still have a timeless appeal and provide one of the most popular themes in decoration.

Surely, then, there is exciting scope for experiment with present design trends, rather than retreating into the past.

An early eighteenth-century child's sampler
The embroidery is in tent-stitch, counted satin and eyelet holes on linen. The embroidered verse reads:

> "Gay dainty flowers go swiftly to decay,
> Poor wretched life's short portion flies away,
> We eat, we drink, we sleep, but lo, anon,
> Old age steals on us never thought upon."

and is signed: "Mary Wakeling Ended this December The Tenth 1742 Aged Ten Years. . . ."

(By courtesy of the Victoria & Albert Museum. Crown Copyright)

One

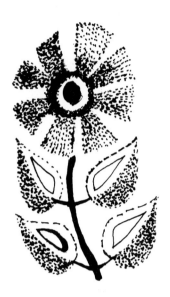

EARLY USE OF PLANT FORMS
IN DECORATION

"The actual systems of building pattern, of pattern forms . . . have been discovered
long ago, but it is in their re-combination and adaptation, our interpretation and use
of them, and in the power of variation and expression, that modern invention and
predilection tell. . . ."

Walter Crane, *Bases of Design*.

FROM archaeological discoveries made so far, it is believed that the first textiles were
produced at some period between twelve and twenty thousand years ago, during what is
called the New Stone Age. At first they were roughly woven from plant fibre, and a later
development was the addition of patterning worked into the warp threads with a needle.
This technique is believed to be the very first method used for producing patterned
ornament, and from it, embroidery developed as a later and separate craft. The small
number of early embroideries extant today, mostly discovered in tombs and burial places,
survive from times when the craft was already ancient, but despite lack of evidence we may
assume that styles of decoration applied to robes and hangings in the ancient world were
similar to those embellishing the pottery, sculpture, architecture and mural paintings of the
same period, and this is borne out by the representations of figures wearing embroidered
garments which frequently feature as themes for ornament themselves.

The invention of needles preceded that of cloth by some thousands of years. Bone
needles were among the tools of the later Paleolithic people, who existed perhaps thirty

thousand years ago. H. G. Wells, in his *Short History of the World*, quotes de Mortillet as saying, "The bone needles of this Age are much superior to those of later, even historical times, down to the Renaissance. The Romans, for example, never had needles comparable to those of this epoch."

Plant form in Prehistoric Art

Egyptian Amratian. (Azilian Period?) 12000–15000 B.C.

Geometric patterns and floral and other devices were scratched on these implements. They were not intended to decorate, but to express symbolic ideas connected with religious ritual. The use of natural forms solely as decoration was a later development, when symbolic meaning had become subordinated to aesthetic expression. All decorative art in ancient times was highly symbolic. Primitive man took from Nature familiar living things and invested them with magical powers, some benign, others war-like and retributive. The ritualistic importance of plants and flowers must have become established following the development of agriculture in Neolithic times, when community life became bound up with the seasons, and religious ritual centred on the cycle of sowing and harvesting.

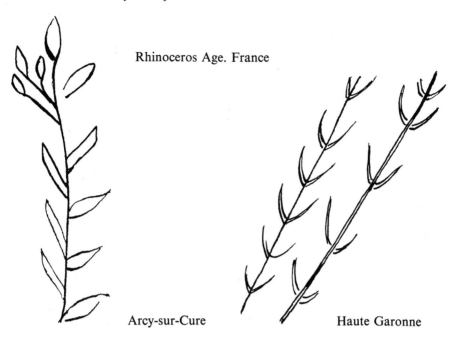

Rhinoceros Age. France

Arcy-sur-Cure   Haute Garonne

In the modern world it is hard to imagine how unprotected against the elements our ancestors were, and how stark and uncomfortable life must have been. Small wonder that the advent of spring, with easier living, and the hope of a good harvest, was celebrated by elaborate rites and ceremonies. The reappearance of flowers at this time would give them a special significance. The wearing of garlands is associated with most ancient primitive rituals, and today flowers still play an accepted part in social functions of every kind. Ornamenting with flowers, either living, or through the medium of art, symbolised importance. That which was ornamented took on added virtue—it became an object of esteem. From this original idea, plants have been a constant source of decorative inspiration, perhaps to a greater and more universal extent than any other aspect of Nature. For even when shorn of their ancient significance, it is difficult to imagine any other natural forms which lend themselves so readily as ornament, or which have such a wide range of appropriate application in art.

Throughout the centuries floral ornament continuously changed or modified its forms. It was influenced by foreign elements due to trade, shifting populations and military conquest. Frequently, devices that had outworn their original roles were modified to serve other functions, a process that Professor Christie has called "the regeneration of decadent material in new forms" . . . Floral motifs also changed with constant repetition, although some, dedicated to religious use in the remote past, have occasionally survived almost unaltered down to our own time. As a result of the spreading of religions and migration of populations it is found that types of flower occur in the ornamental arts of countries in which they may not be indigenous. The people of countries whose climate was especially favourable to the growing of flowers, such as India, Persia, Syria and the Far East, already highly civilised while Europe was emerging from barbarism, reflect this natural profusion in all their decorative art. The plant forms of India and Persia especially attained a degree of refinement and artistry earlier than anything found in Europe.

The plants represented in prehistoric art are supposed to have had a remote allegorical significance, and not to have imparted magical powers in the same way as animal forms. Archaeological excavations have traced the periods and manner in which floral devices spread and were adapted from one region to another, and the stages of modification which they underwent.

Lily:
Naturalistic. Knossos, Crete, 2000 B.C. Later becoming more formalised

The lily appeared in Crete about 2000 B.C. represented quite naturalistically, but by about 1400 B.C. it had become highly formalised. Next, it spread to Syria, where by 1370 B.C. it was being treated in a botanical manner with all the parts distinguished. This form appeared in other countries, down to the Hittite form, at which point the Assyrians produced their formalised bowl type. From here, the lily passed through various western stages, and ultimately a thousand years of classical change, until it finally disappeared.

Formal. Late Hellenic: from Korakou

Crete (Tamassos)

Crete (Ialysos), 1450 B.C.

Crete (Ialysos), 1400 B.C.

from Knossos

Fleur-de-lys:
Formalised. Crete (Knossos), 1500 B.C.

Late Hellenic. Crete (Korakou)

There is some disagreement over the significance of the lotus and papyrus flowers which appear so often in Ancient Egyptian and Assyrian art. One opinion asserts that they were used purely for decoration, as objects beautiful in themselves. Other authorities think that they possessed minor religious significance. Actually, the ancient Egyptians were great garden lovers, like the people of Tudor England so many centuries later. The blue lotus was their favourite flower, and it was worn so frequently as an adornment that it became virtually part of the native dress. The lotus motif spread to Greece, and from there to Rome and the West, and later became symbolically associated with Buddhism.

Decorative Lotus design painted
on blue faience hippo,
circa 1600 B.C.

Egyptian Lotus, 1450 B.C.

Mural painting of
sacred cat
with papyrus,
circa 1900 B.C.

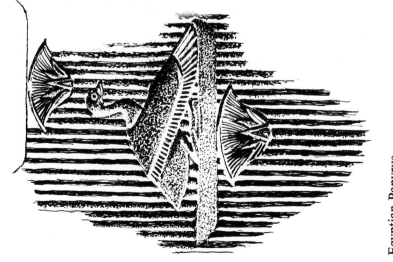

Egyptian Papyrus.
Relief carving in limestone with duck on nest,
circa 2650 B.C.

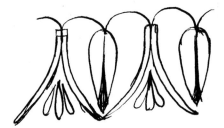

Variations of the Lotus: from Rhodes

Assyrian Lotus from Nimrud embroidery

Assyria (Kouyunjik)

However, it was the date-palm which provided one of the richest sources of imaginative symbolism in ancient and classical times—the Tree of Life, that in remote antiquity provided food and shelter, and the first fermented drink. Among primitive peoples the palm was an emblem of fertility, being later adopted as the Christian symbol of peace and the Resurrection. In the pre-Christian era it is represented by highly conventionalised palm foliage. The palm was brought into Egypt by 2800 B.C. and spread from there to Assyria where it is found on the capitals of columns, and in running borders. The Greeks combined it with the acanthus leaf, and later it was modified by other floral elements, such as the lotus and the lily, into the traditional palmette form. A version of this, the "split palmette", may have been the prototype of the Greek anthemion, or honeysuckle.

Another device more closely associated with embroidery was the pine or cone, representing the male pollen-bearing palm flower. This is seen in the ornament of Persia, Egypt and Palestine, and especially in the textiles and embroideries of India, where it is sometimes known as the "mango" device, being rather similar in form to that fruit. It appears in English "chinoiserie" embroideries, and Paisley shawls, which are copied from the traditional designs of Kashmir, are almost all based on pattern arrangements of the cone.

Variations of the Cone device from Indian Textiles

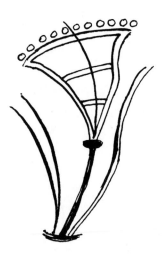

Variations of the Pink: from Palaikastro

Pink from Knossos

Vetch.
Early Greek naturalistic

Olive. Mid Apulia

Star Anemone. Palaikastro

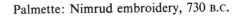

Palmette: Nimrud embroidery, 730 B.C.

Palm: from Pylos Maia

Early ornament was based on geometric principles, constructed from curves and angles, and conforming to their restrictions. It first took the form of decorative bands. Later these bands were grouped together to create all-over pattern. As plants and flowers were utilised in decoration, their arrangement passed through various phases of expression, geometric, abstract, or conventional-naturalistic, according to the time in which they were being used, forming separate and distinct styles, so that we inherit a complex grammar of ornament which contains elements derived from very ancient and diffuse sources. There are certain types of basic arrangement, for example, whose essentials were defined at an early date in the history of ornament, and to at least one of which any modern interpretation must in some way be linked. This is why it is true to say that absolute originality in art is not possible—we can differ from our forefathers only in inventiveness.

The classical *scroll* arrangement is based on the spiral, which dates back before the Neolithic age to the Azilian Period, 12000–15000 B.C. It is one of the most important elements in decoration, superbly used in Egyptian, Byzantine and Greek ornament, and has many related forms, such as the Wave, the Undulating, the Meander, etc., the basic principle of all these forms being the circle. In Tudor embroidery, scrolled stems framing single flower heads were a popular style of all-over patterning. When plant forms are represented in this way, their methods of organic growth have to be extremely formalised, or even ignored, and the plant treated in a conventionalised or abstract manner.

Crocus. Formal. Cycladic

Crocus: from Therka

In *arabesque* ornament, the geometric principle is not so apparent. The arabesque form appeared about 300 B.C. as a more ornate representation of the scroll, beginning with a bract at the fork of a branch developing into a calyx form. This arrangement became freer and more flowing, and later included quaint creatures, vase shapes and grotesques. It is typified in the work of the Italian Renaissance, which Robert Adam so admired, and copied in his interiors, although in England, Arabesque never developed into the extreme rococo style that it did elsewhere. Broadly speaking, the trend in all art has been from severity and repose in the early periods, to greater freedom and movement in the later.

Arabesque form. Graeco-Roman, 300 B.C.:
from Tuneh

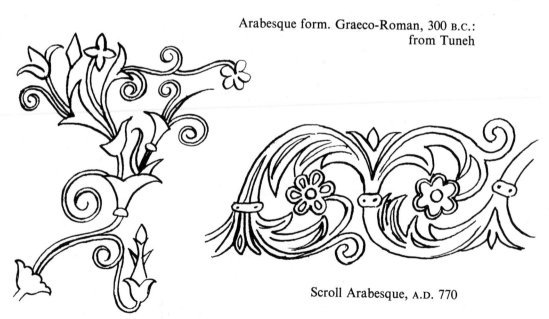

Scroll Arabesque, A.D. 770

In addition to these methods of rhythmic arrangement, there are traditional ways in which floral design may be imposed on ground fabric as embroidered ornament. Either as *self-contained* design, composed for the purpose of filling a particular space: a *repeating* design, such as a border repeating in two directions only, or a continuous *all-over pattern* repeating in all directions; a *geometric diaper* pattern, where the repeat is frequent and small in scale to the area covered, as in blackwork; a sprig pattern, or *random diaper*, where the ground is scattered with small isolated motifs not necessarily repeating; or a combination of two or more of these types of imposition. There are, of course, many other pattern forms inappropriate for embroidery.

Embroidered floral decoration is only one aspect of this universal ornamental theme which forms one of the most important branches of the applied arts. Here is an instance of floral ornament being used on a glover's tombstone in the churchyard of Brightwell Baldwin in Oxon., in a manner that is both simple and charming.

(*Taken from an original lithograph by Clarke Hutton*)

Chinese nineteenth-century sleeve band
The embroidery is in shades of blue, green, ochre and rust silk, on blue silk fabric. The stitches mostly Chinese knot-stitch, with a little couched metal thread. A self-contained design.
(*By courtesy of the Needlework Development Scheme*)

Nineteenth-century Austrian embroidered border
Worked in thick pink and black cotton on a white linen ground. The stitches are satin, feather, French knots, stem and lattice fillings and the treatment is perfectly flat, formalised and boldly decorative, using two tones only. A symmetrical design.
(*By courtesy of the Needlework Development Scheme*)

Turkish tambour embroidery
Using silk and metal threads on natural coloured silk material, the embroidery in a range of soft greens, fawns and blues. A self-contained design repeated to make an all-over pattern.

(*By courtesy of the Needlework Development Scheme*)

Two

PRINCIPLES OF DESIGN

"Ornament depends upon craftsmanship for its physical existence; but design is the intellectual motive power behind the technique which gives it expression. Technique, when properly respected, is a good servant to design, but never its master. . . ."
A. H. Christie, *Traditional Methods of Pattern Designing.*

THE final aim of any design should be *unity*, that certain quality of completeness brought about through the co-operation of every aspect of a decorative idea—design, colour, material, method and function. There are certain artistic rules which must be observed if this is to be achieved. Our laws of design are derived from those in Nature, and though we may do so unconsciously, we use Nature as our ideal standard for judging art. There is, in fact, no man-made pattern or structural arrangement whose prototype does not occur in Nature, in whom we see the endless reiteration of those fundamental geometric forms with which everyone is familiar—the spiral, the cone, the ellipse, the circle, and so on, which underlie all forms in art. Design might be accurately described as an ordered arrangement of separate forms controlled by geometrical relationships. But although geometry is the basis of design, it is not possible to design purely by it. It is true that the designer is concerned with composing shapes and masses into what is essentially an abstruse mathematical relationship, but she must be guided not by instruments or calculations but by her own eye, and her sense of proportion and fitness. The ultimate success or otherwise of the design must obviously depend on the degree to which her artistic sense is developed, combined with her appreciation of fundamental principles.

1. PROPORTION. This is the satisfactory relationship in scale between all the varied

32

units composing a design, and between the design itself and its adjoining areas of un-decorated ground fabric. Good proportion must always be closely associated with balance, and inseparable from function. Its laws have been extensively studied in terms of mathematics and philosophy. The ancient Greeks established a theory of perfect proportion, the "Golden Mean", based on definite geometric formulae, and observed certain ratios of measurement in their art and architecture designed to achieve the utmost balance, harmony and satisfaction to the eye.

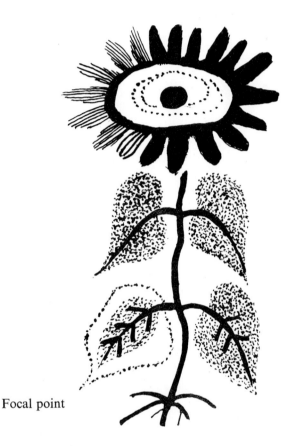

Focal point

2. FOCAL POINT. A focal point or centre of interest is a necessary element in a design, to which all other parts are related. This means emphasising certain parts of the design and understressing others to just the right degree. The physical eye needs this stimulus when viewing any work of art, the first visual impact being made at the focal point, and the vision then, as it were, circling round the whole design and coming back to rest at the original point. Lacking this, a design will tend to become a monotonous rambling pattern of shapes, without coherence. A focal point in embroidery can be achieved by using a different thickness of thread, or introducing a contrasting colour or texture, a variation in scale, a sudden change of stitch, or by a combination of all these methods.

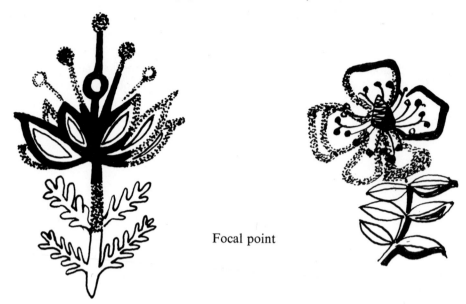

Focal point

3. BALANCE. We observe this everywhere in Nature, and in art it is maintained by the complementary relationship of all the opposite elements composing a design. The question of balance is especially important in plant design, as the nature of a plant tends to make it top-heavy. In Nature the construction of plants may be either symmetrical or asymmetrical, but even when asymmetrical, it is such that an *impression* of symmetry is produced, and this is what is meant by balance. A good example may be observed in trees, where although the individual branches are asymmetrical, balance is preserved by their general distribution.

Balance

Balance

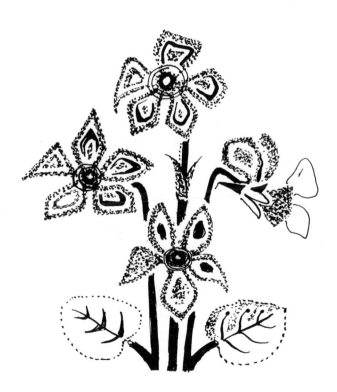

Balance

4. RHYTHM. This is an essential quality in design which cannot really be taught but must be innate. In Nature it is demonstrated in every aspect of plant growth. The dictionary defines rhythm as a "measured flow, or cadence". It is not necessarily linked with symmetry, neither is it demonstrated merely by the use of wavy swinging lines, which indeed, if used to excess in any design, will be a weakening factor. Rhythm is really an intangible quality, expressed in the co-ordination of all the elements composing a design, something which is not imposed from the outside, but reflected in the total work.

The foregoing are *qualities*, whose relationship with each other are requisite for good design. Two others exist, with which the designer must also be preoccupied, and these are harmony and contrast. *Harmony* in a design is the quality of peace and orderliness obtained by correct relationship of form and colour. *Contrast* is obtained by combining forms of different character to give variation and liveliness. When contrasting forms or colours are correctly related, however, the result is harmony, so that strictly speaking the principal ingredient of harmony is the correct use of contrast. A harmonious design should give a feeling of calmness and repose without monotony.

Rhythm

Rhythm

A design is composed of lines and shapes, all of which simultaneously contribute their own particular statements and values within it, and produce on us definite sensations. The fundamental components of design are straight lines and forms combined with curving ones, each complementing the other, because the former supply strength and stability to the design, and the latter give grace and flexibility, but are also a weakening element. A design composed of a majority of curving lines and shapes is therefore likely to be flabby and indecisive unless these are complemented by the addition of firm straight ones; it may also be unpleasantly restless. This is important to remember when dealing with plant forms.

Straight lines and straight-sided shapes reflect the laws of gravity, hence their dominance over curving ones. Vertical straight lines have vitality and force, while horizontal lines have the property of repose. An oblique line or form emphasises the pull of gravity, and must be counterbalanced by thrust in an opposing direction. This *direction of thrust* is a most important factor in design, and when plants are studied it will be seen that their growth patterns are composed of perfectly balanced thrust and counter-thrust.

Direction of thrust

Upward growth

Upward growth

It is unnecessary to add that the principles which have been outlined here are basically architectural. They have been observed from the very beginning of created design, and the history of art from the time of classical Greece is a record of the variations in style produced in each period by the stressing of one or more of these principles, and the subordination of others. Any attempt, however, to design purely by the application of theory will produce at best a mechanical and uninspired result. Design is much more than the observance of a set of rules, it is a means of self-expression in which the emotions must be involved; in fact it is a personal experience, different for each individual. An artist of exceptional ability may well take liberties with accepted principles if so desired, and yet achieve success through sheer mastery of the medium. The rules governing design have to be applied unconsciously while the worker is grappling consciously with her problems of colour, texture and stitchery. Only by understanding them can she criticise her own work (which she must do) and recognise good and bad design among the everyday objects surrounding her.

Bedroom mules

Worked on the domestic sewing-machine. The material from which they are made is French-grey crêpe-de-chine, and the embroidery is in self-colour, also black, yellow and dark red.

The stitching is in free running, zig-zag and satin-stitch, and the soles and toe-sections are quilted. The decoration is quite symmetrical, the construction of the slipper being utilised as part of the design.

Designed and embroidered by LILIAN WILLEY.

(*By courtesy of the Needlework Development Scheme*)

Pencil study of a rose by Richard Addington
(*By courtesy of the Needlework Development Scheme*)

Embroidered adaptation of the Addington rose drawing, on dark almond-green ribbed rayon fabric, with the embroidery carried out in white felt appliqué with silver metal thread and various thicknesses of cotton threads in fawn, white, beige and different greens. Stitches are satin-stitch laid work, couching, back-stitch and French knots. For embroidering it was necessary to spread out and flatten the leaves and also eliminate some of the detail in the rose itself.

Interpretation by the AUTHOR.

(*By courtesy of the Needlework Development Scheme*)

A second interpretation of the Addington rose, adapted for use as a repeating motif for a counter-pane. The design and treatment are similar, but the felt appliqué is replaced by hemmed appliqué in olive-green satin, and the silver metal thread with silver and white rayon and floss silk threads. Other colours in different thicknesses of cotton threads include grey, emerald, yellow-green, black, citron and a little crimson.

   Interpretation by the AUTHOR.

(*By courtesy of the Needlework Development Scheme*)

The completed counterpane made of dark almond-green ribbed rayon, decorated with embroidered rose motifs arranged so that they will appear as far as possible on the surface of the bed. There are two different adaptations of the original drawing used, and though all the motifs are embroidered in the same colour range, the colours are differently grouped for each, to avoid monotony. They are emerald, turquoise and various greens, fawn, beige, cream, citron, black, white and grey, with small amounts of crimson. The counterpane is edged with bands of dull turquoise satin.

Designed and made by the AUTHOR.

(*By courtesy of the Needlework Development Scheme*)

A tea-cosy
Made from pale yellow linen with embroidery in various cotton threads in black, cream, grey-green and touches of pink contrast. The stitches include couching, stem, double knot, sheaf-stitch, flat-stitch and French knots. The cosy is finished with black piping.

    Designed and embroidered by MARGARET WILSON.

(By courtesy of the Needlework Development Scheme)

An evening bag

Hand-embroidered in silk thread on oyster satin in subtle pinks, greys, cream and yellow, with touches of crimson and green. The stitches used include satin-stitch, French knots, back-stitch and couching.

A delightful, free design adapted from a motif on an Ayrshire christening robe, and enhanced by the more varied treatment which is made possible by its different technical interpretation.

Design by HELEN STREVENS, embroidery by JOAN WHAYMAN, layout and making-up by MARGARET WILSON.

(*By courtesy of the Needlework Development Scheme*)

Three

METHODS OF NATURAL GROWTH
TRANSLATION INTO FLAT DECORATION

"To the artist, a different treatment is as good as a different plant."
Richard Hatton, *The Craftsman's Plant Book*.

IT is really desirable to study from the actual living plant, to observe from every angle individual styles of growth, and to recognise the separate forms and personalities of flowers. Botanical drawings are particularly useful in that they dissect and clarify general plant structure and enable the designer to build up a wealth of floral forms which will be invaluable reference.

Some flowers are obviously unsuited for embroidery. The worker will learn from her studies which are the most suitable types—those in which the characteristics of growth and construction are simple and easily seen, and whose shapes are well defined and lend themselves to conventionalisation. The influencing factors for the designer are the qualities and limitations of her medium, which is fabric and thread. Flowers that are spidery or fussy in their structure do not adapt themselves readily to embroidery. The designer will find it is more difficult to make a simple design from a complicated flower than an elaborate design from a simple one. The process is primarily one of searching out the main shapes of the flower by which it is truly characterised and simplifying or omitting such others which, although part of the actual plant, if included will cause the design to become overloaded with detail and difficult to read. Even where a recognisable likeness of a flower is required, the design is still more important than the subject, meaning that the finished result should

48

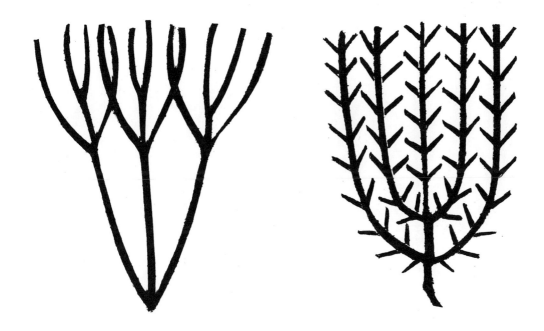

Patterns of plant growth

be Nature translated into art, not art attempting to imitate Nature. In some cases it may be desirable deliberately to exaggerate certain parts of the flower which are actually subordinate within its general structure, or to rearrange others, if this helps the design; in fact there are progressive degrees of abstraction by which it is possible to compose a natural flower into an embroidered flower. The personal skill of the worker is reflected in the forms she selects or rejects, and the manner in which she expresses them through her medium. Every design is a law unto itself, and according to the method of working to be employed, so must the designer vary her degree of conventionalisation—her modification from naturalistic to ornamental, and she must bear in mind also that the flower itself is but one aspect of the whole design, and that stem, leaves and sometimes roots are equally important.

Patterns of plant growth

Patterns of plant growth

The whole basis of flower design is observation of the way in which plants grow, and the innumerable patterns of their growth, their various external shapes, and the arrangement of their leaves and general underlying structure. Plant growth is based on three natural principles. The first is *radiation*, which is the spreading out of lines or forms from a point of common origin, as in the petals of flowers and vein structure of some types of leaf. The second is known as *tangential junction*, which is closely associated with radiation, and is the springing of leaves, branches, roots and tendrils from the parent stem. The embroiderer should make a particular study of the ways in which branches, stems, leaves and flowers are attached to the main stalk of the plant, as lack of observation at these points frequently leads to weakness in the design. These two principles are complementary elements, as the former will produce harmony and repose and the latter energy and movement. The third is the principle of *tapering*, or decrease of stem thickness relative to the scale of growth with which it is associated.

Plants convey a feeling of springing upward and outward, and a floral design should not lose this vital quality even though its total effect must be one of balance and repose. The embroiderer, if she cares to look, cannot fail to discover for herself the way in which this plant-growth characteristic has been expressed in the decorative arts of the past, and to see how artists in their different ways have approached the problems of simplification in order to obtain the kind of silhouette best suited to their particular medium.

Studies from the living plant

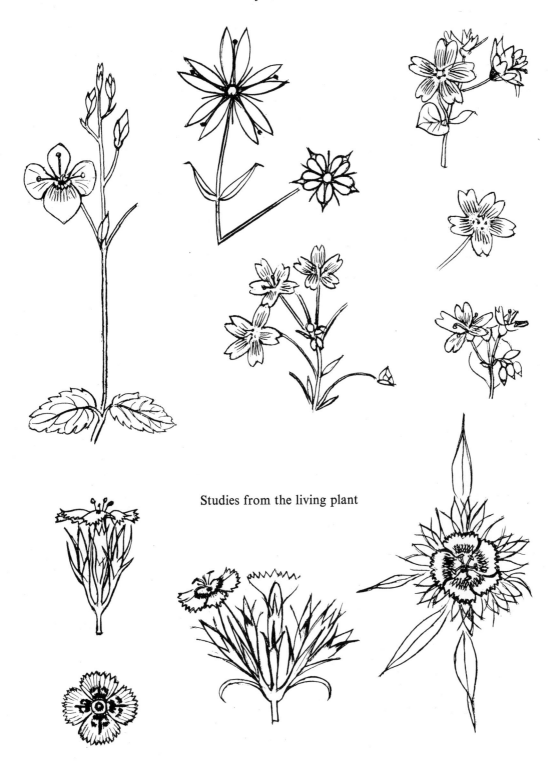

Studies from the living plant

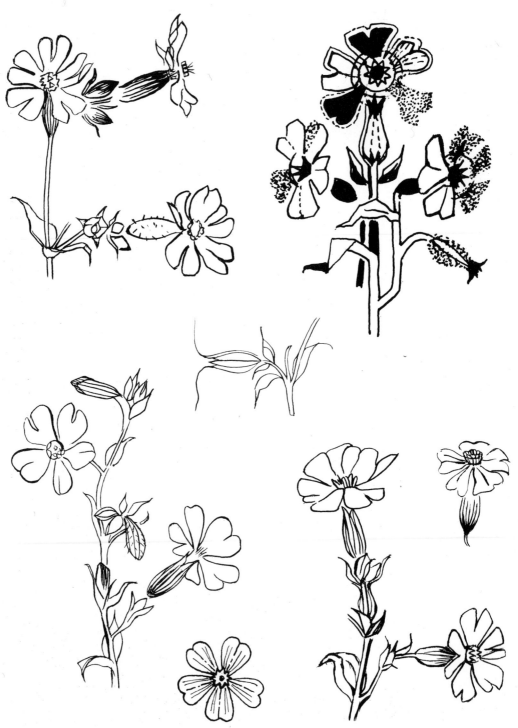

Studies from the living plant—Campion

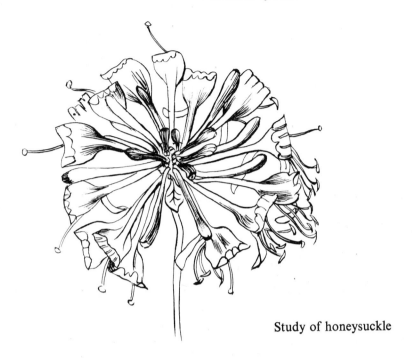

Study of honeysuckle

Simplified idea of honeysuckle

Study of honeysuckle

Simplified idea of honeysuckle

Stages of formalisation:
(*a*) Semi-naturalistic with
mainly curving forms

(*b*) Simplified sketch —
some parts removed,
and forms straight-
ened

(*c*) Stiffened formalised
treatment with
straightening of
forms. Some parts
detached

Formalising

Enlarging and reducing by means of the common diagonal

Cover for a blotter

The ground material is fine black cotton, and the embroidery is carried out in hemmed cotton appliqué over paper templates, and various thicknesses of cotton threads. Stitches used are couching, chain-stitch, running and feather-stitch.

The colours include grey, blue-grey, olive-green, red, cream, yellow, beige and white. The floral motifs are purely flat and decorative in treatment, expressed by means of geometric shapes based on primitive designs. Excessive stiffness has been counteracted where necessary by freely worked outlines.

Adapted by the AUTHOR from an original embroidery by PATRICIA BREARLEY. Making-up by JESSIE DUNN.

(*By courtesy of the Needlework Development Scheme*)

Formalising

Unit composed into border motif

Central European linen shirt

Probably nineteenth century, embroidered in blue, wine, yellow and black cross-stitch. A fine example of a geometric all-over repeating design on the counted thread.

The pattern is built up from a series of repeating border strips worked side by side, in which individual motifs are less important than their relationship to each other and the intervening spaces between them. The total effect is even and harmonious.

(*By courtesy of the Needlework Development Scheme*)

Simplification is indeed the essential ingredient of flower embroidery. It must be insisted that the object of the embroiderer is not to illustrate a seed catalogue, or even necessarily to produce a recognisable species of flower, but firstly to express the essence of all flowers and only secondly to represent, if so desired, the predominant characteristics of one particular sort. The degree of flattening and formalising required will inevitably necessitate liberties having to be taken with surface form, perhaps the detachment of some parts from the rest, or the understressing of certain areas. A skilful designer composes her design so that the eye of the viewer makes its own unconscious contribution, the fraction she deliberately leaves unsaid being paradoxically often one of the telling factors in design. The element of understatement is as highly effective in embroidery as it is in other arts.

In a design containing floral forms of similar species, variation in shape, treatment and possibly scale is desirable. This may be quite slight but it will avoid monotonous repetition.

In Nature no flower or plant is *exactly* like another flower or plant of the same species, and no flowers or leaves are identical even on the same plant, and in this respect art may safely imitate Nature. The foregoing does not, however, necessarily apply in the case of the repeating border or all-over pattern whose purpose is to provide enrichment of a different category from that of isolated or self-contained design. Each unit of a repeating design, being less important than its relationship with all the other units making up the pattern, may be complete in itself, but must not be obtrusive.

Cover for an address book
The embroidery is in tones of green-blue and purple on a panel of pink silk, mounted on to dull grey corded silk.

An interpretation of a composite flower, bell heather. The arrangement and varied shapes of the individual florets are interestingly contrasted, and at the same time they are composed together to create a sensitive and balanced design.

The embroidery is carried out in back-stitch, detached chain, stem-stitch and French knots.

Designed and embroidered by HELEN STREVENS. Making-up by IRIS HILLS.

(*By courtesy of the Needlework Development Scheme*)

A machine-embroidered evening bag

The decoration being an interpretation of a chalk drawing by MARY KESSELL. One of the pieces made for an experiment in embroidery design sponsored by the Needlework Development Scheme between 1946–9.

The bag is worked entirely in free running on the domestic sewing-machine, the speed and fluidity of the machine stitching admirably reproducing the spontaneous abstract feeling of the design, while adding a pleasant texture of its own.

The bag is white corded silk, lined with pink georgette, and the embroidery is in tones of red, rust, pink, grey and blue.

Embroidered and made by FRANCES BEAL from an adaptation of the original Kessell drawing by LILIAN WILLEY.

(*By courtesy of the Needlework Development Scheme*)

Finger-plate

Worked on the domestic sewing-machine.

The motif is embroidered on white organdie in blues and greens. A shadow effect is obtained by placing another motif behind it. The design is beautifully balanced and adapted to fit its rectangular shape.

Designed and embroidered by LILIAN WILLEY.

Finger-plate

The embroidery is in a restrained scheme of yellow-greens, the ground olive-green taffeta.

Stitches include couching, coral knot, chain, back-stitch, running and French knots. The design is predominantly linear; variations in line thickness give it richness and stability.

Designed by HELEN STREVENS.
Embroidered by MARGARET WILSON.

(By courtesy of the Needlework Development Scheme)

Madonna lily

Embroidered for centre panel of Festival frontal in Bromley Parish Church, Kent.

The background material is a French cream silk brocade with 12½ in. pattern repeat. The height of the lily 22 in. and the dimension of panel 2 ft. 6 in. square. The embroidery worked in raised and flat laid gold, gold basket filling, and silk and satin appliqué in tones of gold and buff. Raised and flat satin-stitch and laid fillings in floss and purse silks, with couched hand-made cord outlines.

The direction of the "grain" in each portion of appliqué is placed to ensure an equal balance of toning when subjected to an angled view. The scale of working is fairly bold to suit the size of the motif. No attempt has been made to render the lily naturalistically; it is treated quite formally as a symmetrical design.

From an original layout by PATRICIA ROOKE, developed and embroidered by the AUTHOR.

(*By courtesy of the Vicar of Bromley*)

Four

TREATMENT OF FLOWERS IN DESIGN

"We see in needleworkes and embroideries it is more pleasing to have a lively work upon a sad and solemn ground than to have a dark and melancholy work upon a lightsome ground. . . ."

Sir Francis Bacon, 1561–1626, in his essay *Of Adversity*.

THE essence of embroidery lies in its textile quality—its validity as an arrangement of fabrics and threads, and the feeling of permanence, of completeness, that it conveys. Present trends demand a lighter, freer style of expression than in the past. Victorian-style naturalism, its flower themes rendered as embroidered portraits, with no attempt at arrangement into formal decoration, practises a deception by trying to give the illusion of reality. The function of embroidery is to be itself, not imitation painting or photography. Decorative art should be flat and free from perspective, since whatever it adorns will have shapes and contours to which the decoration is subordinate, and which it must not attempt to falsify. Mrs Christie, in her introductory chapter to *Samplers and Stitches*, says: ". . . However pleasing exact imitation may be it is not a high form of art; it is a mistake in embroidery, as in all decorative art, to be realistic. To absorb and transform the real is the true function of art. The avoidance of realism is a question of design as well as technique, for the two cannot but go hand in hand. Naturalistic treatment of floral designs is best avoided by the worker with the needle; there is a place for nature and one for art, and when nature is adapted to artistic uses it needs a certain formalism to make it suit its artificial environment . . ."[1]

[1] *Samplers and Stitches*, Mrs Archibald Christie (B. T. Batsford Ltd, 1920).

68

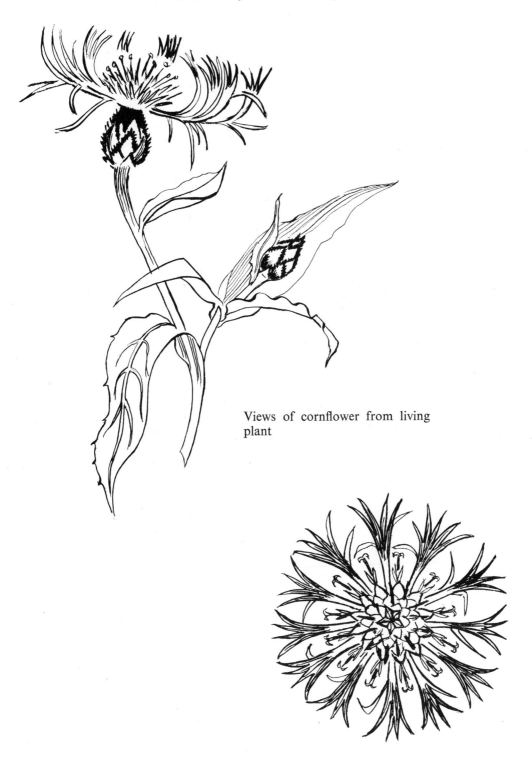

Views of cornflower from living
plant

The cornflower drawing in process
of modification as an idea for
surface stitchery including appliqué (represented by shaded areas)

The same motif arranged for canvas embroidery, formalised and geometrical with its various parts extremely simplified

A method of free treatment possible to obtain with the sewing-machine

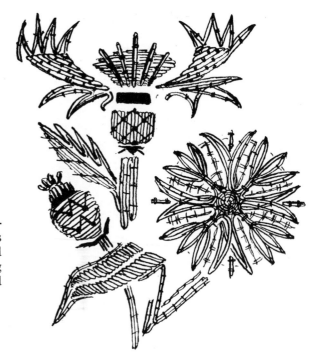

Two further possibilities for different treatments: the cornflower as it might be interpreted in gold thread and silk, mainly in couching and a little satin-stitch and laid work

An idea for shadow-work. This method may be enhanced by the addition of a little fine line surface stitchery

The cornflower motif is shown
here adapted for blackwork with
suggested variations of treatment

The concern of embroidery is not with direct ideas. This is the province of the fine arts—of painting and sculpture. The proper function of embroidery is in the expression of form, such ideas as there may be being interpreted by means of symbols, expressed by form and pattern. Embroidery by its very nature is restricted to symbolism, and is not a medium for interpreting emotion. This is the essential difference between the major and minor arts. Any attempt by embroidery to ignore the emotional detachment imposed upon it by its own limited means of expression, at best can only result in an uneasy mixing of applied and fine art characteristics, which if carried to extremes will produce a kind of non-art hybrid, without meaning or value.

Flowers must be adapted for embroidery from three-dimensional form into flat shapes. This process of translation from three-dimensional to two-dimensional is agreed to be one of the most difficult problems which designers have to face, and this is why flowers are among the hardest things to interpret successfully in embroidery, and are so quickly desecrated in the hands of an insensitive worker. To produce good floral embroidery, there must first of all be love and understanding of the subject. If the worker does not really care about flowers and has merely adopted one for lack of any other creative idea, there is little doubt that her finished work will reflect this attitude. There is a greater danger, however, that her interpretation may become oversentimental, a quality which is highly undesirable in needlework. The fact that the shapes she is using represent flowers, can never excuse weakness or sentimentality; the embroiderer's job is to discover the essence of her flower, and re-create it into a design which expresses its structure and captures its individual personality in such a way as to produce an unmistakable floral form, while yet avoiding naturalism. The stitchery should be subordinate to the design in that it must be a medium of expression, a means to an end and not an end in itself. A good design will shine through indifferent technique, whereas a bad design cannot be disguised by good technique, but will, in fact, be shown up all the more obviously by it. The ultimate stage of technique worship is the reduction of a piece of work to a mere exercise in manual dexterity, the character and personality of the worker extinguished in chilly perfection.

The worker who has a large repertoire of stitches needs to beware of introducing too great a variety into her embroidery and destroying the unity of the design. It is not the variety of stitches employed, but the manner in which the few necessary to express the worker's intention are used, which will produce a good piece of work. Today's trend towards spontaneity calls for a free, direct and simplified manner of working surface methods, and some of the more intricate and ornate stitches are obviously inappropriate in modern embroidery, unless used with great discretion. We have to recognise that some modes of embroidery have by now largely lost their meaning, and become mere technical exercises out of tune with the present day, but on the other hand, others must surely have received fresh stimulus from the wealth of intriguing new fabrics on the market, many of which invite new ideas for interesting stitch treatment.

Embroidered flowers express the characteristics of the particular methods in which they are worked, and there must be an understanding of the potentialities of these methods on the part of the worker, if her interpretation is to succeed. Surface methods of embroidery give greater fluency and opportunity for experiment in textural and colour contrasts, by

Building up tone harmony using cut paper

means of applied materials, and the use of varying weights of thread. Apart from the necessary relationship of design to material, and material to function, there will be less discipline imposed by the ground fabric than in counted-thread methods. Surface embroidery is, therefore, ideally suited to expressing the free design style of today.

The formal geometric character of counted-thread embroidery can, however, be extremely decorative and satisfying. Counted-thread methods impose severer limitations on the worker, and require a simpler and flatter type of design, and it is necessary for flowers so interpreted to be translated into as few and simple shapes as possible. The problem for the designer is to re-create her flower shapes so as to be still recognisable as flowers, despite the conventionalism imposed on her by the medium. Sketching on squared paper is invaluable in the early stages, as without this, it is easy to produce a kind of distorted naturalism. With increasing experience, she will learn how to exploit to best advantage the method in which she is working, without forcing it beyond what it will effectively do.

The general appearance of any piece of embroidery should be flat, but a close scrutiny of the separate stitches composing it reveals that as well as possessing individual differences of form and contour, the way they are constructed with the needle causes each to lie in a certain characteristic way, either open and rounded, or with a vertical, horizontal or oblique direction of thrust. An experienced worker consciously utilises this "stitch-direction" and without doubt it is one of the important factors contributing to sensitive and intelligent embroidery, especially where the method used entails the use of solid fillings, such as canvas-work. Here, clever choice of stitch-direction may well play a more essential part than colour in defining the main shapes of the design and their relationship, and provide contrasts of surface texture which make an important contribution to the general effect. Since embroidery is the expression of form through stitchery, it can be understood that an inspired use of stitches may help to elucidate a vague design, but on the other hand, the proportion and balance of a strong clear form can be seriously upset, even nullified, by the use of a stitch whose own direction and general effect is in conflict with that form.

Cut paper is a quick and free method of reducing a design to the essentials of flat decoration, and if used intelligently can be extremely helpful in several ways. By using this method, the designer is compelled to simplify and flatten her shapes, and to visualise the whole design two-dimensionally. It enables her to experiment with different arrangements of her shapes in relation to each other, so that she can observe how each of their values alters according to their position. It makes her aware how important the actual silhouette of each shape is, in the total design. With black, white and tones of grey paper, she can experiment to produce a satisfactory balance of tone-values, from which a colour scheme can be developed.

The designer should use paper which is fairly firm to handle, such as sugar or cartridge paper. It is a good idea to work through a series of exercises with cut paper, beginning with the simplest type of single flower, and progressing to more elaborate compositions of solid areas, lines and textures, which will help her to acquaint herself with the broad general principles of decorative design. At first, petal and leaf shapes can be cut out quite freely and pasted down to form a bold arrangement which is then built up with added lines.

The designer at this stage is not trying to make an *embroidery* design, she is experimenting with lines in relation to masses. Even when, later, her cut paper compositions can become more controlled and sophisticated, they may serve her as a guide but seldom as an exact replica. It must always be borne in mind that designing for embroidery on paper, or, as in this case, by means of cut paper shapes, although very necessary, is, strictly speaking, only the means of recording ideas during the search for a solution to the problem of expression, and the *final* design lies in the finished work itself, which will have tactile qualities, and an association with its surroundings, incommunicable through the agency of any other medium.

Tone contrast achieved with cut paper

Free cut-paper design with added lines

Free cut-paper design

Simple tone distribution using cut paper

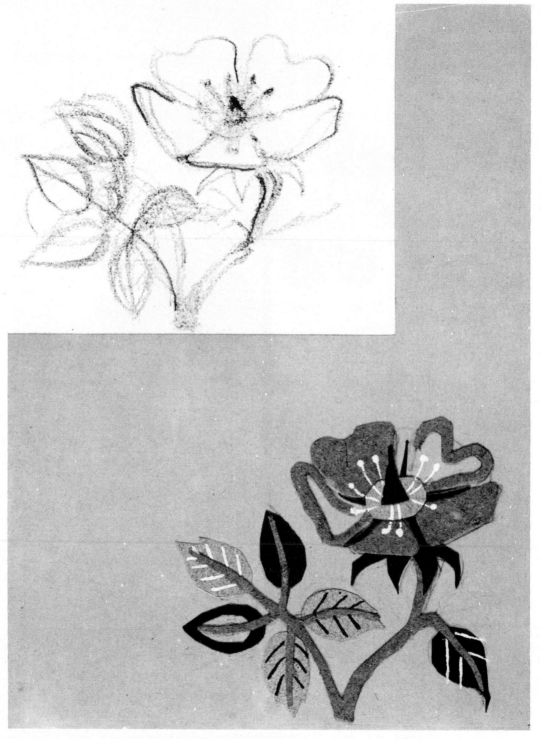

Development of cut-paper motif from original drawing

A wedding veil

Worked on the Irish embroidery machine. The material is cotton net with organdie border and appliqué on the flower and leaf motifs. The stitching includes running, seeding and whip-stitch.

The net is cut away from behind the organdie in some parts of the design, and embroidery worked through both thicknesses in others.

The veil measures 3 sq. yds., and the corner motif covers an area of 1 sq. yd. An example of the delicate tone-values which it is possible to obtain in white work.

Designed and embroidered by MARION W. CAMPBELL.

(*By courtesy of the Designer*)

A child's rag-book

The ground material is pale grey cotton, and the flower motifs are worked mainly in chain-stitch and varieties of chain. The colours are brightly naturalistic. An example of "stitch direction" used to stress form. A single thickness of cotton thread is used for the embroidery.

Designed and embroidered by JEANNE MOUNT.

(*By courtesy of the Needlework Development Scheme*)

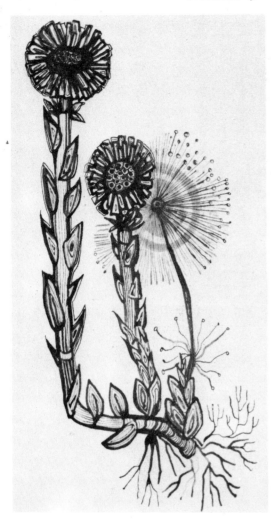 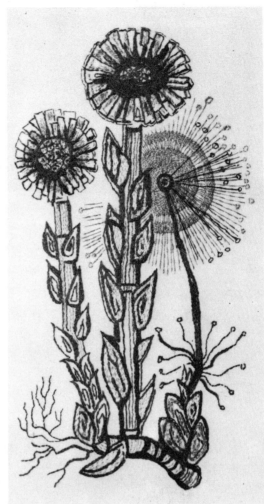

Coltsfoot Designed by HELEN STREVENS.

Left: Freely interpreted in waterproof inks, in tones of blue-grey, sepia, ochre and warm red-brown.

Right: The design adapted for embroidery in a slightly augmented colour-scheme, including pale blue, grey-blue, dark brown, pink, gold, black and touches of deep crimson. The stitches are chain, solid chain filling, back-stitch, split-stitch and French knots.

The original design is modified and re-grouped into a more compact and rectangular arrangement, with the long stem of the left-hand flower shortened for translation in the craft version, where there was a danger that it might appear over-emphasised in relation to the other parts.

Embroidered adaptation by the AUTHOR.

(Both examples by courtesy of the Needlework Development Scheme)

Tone contrast achieved with cut paper

Five

COLOUR

"All sorts of flowers the which on earth doe spring
In goodly colours gloriously array'd."

Edmund Spenser, *c.* 1552–1599.

THE question of colour is one which presents a problem to many of us. We see colour all around us, but the difficulty lies in having to make it ourselves—in changing from spectator to creator, and it is over this change of role that the worker may experience some frustration, especially if she has had little or no formal art training.

The ability to appreciate good colour may not necessarily imply a faculty for creating it, and does not automatically develop with technical skill. A colour-sense is innate, and springs from a natural appreciation of colour observed in everyday life, and where it is latent in an individual it can be stimulated by training. To the physicist colour is a matter of wave-lengths of light; to the physiologist it consists of sensations produced on the retina of the eye; to the artist it is an aspect of form, but more than this, an expression of feeling—an emotional experience; consequently the artistic approach to colour can never be rigidly governed by complicated rules or theories.

An essential condition for the perception of colour is the presence of light. We receive our light from the sun, and sunlight in its purest and most intense form is white light, composed of an infinite number of light waves of varying lengths. The length of each wave determines its colour, and only a relatively small number are visible to the eye. They comprise the group separated out when sunlight is bent or refracted by mist or rain, or by being passed through an optical prism, to form the band of brilliant overlapping colours we know as the solar spectrum. These colours always occur in the same sequence, and if the principal ones are arranged into a circle, a definite relationship between them is at once evident. It is on this relationship that the various modern colour-theories are based, and the colour-circle is useful to the learner-colourist in the same way that an understanding of anatomy is useful to the painter or sculptor, i.e. as a servant but not a master. It must be emphasised again that good colour can never be produced by a mere slavish observance of rules and theories; it relies on much less definable factors, such as personal reaction to the colours seen in nature, the actual colour-sensitivity of the eye, which varies considerably between individuals, and the ability to re-create impressions and sensations which the eye has received. We must not forget that artists were grappling with problems of colour, and solving them, long before Newton discovered the nature of the spectrum in the seventeenth century.

However, in work which involves the use of colour, it is desirable that the worker should be familiar with a little elementary colour-theory, because it can help her to develop her sense of colour discrimination, to correct obvious disharmonies in her colour-schemes, and is also valuable if she wishes to obtain a special colour effect.

The colour-circle is composed of spectral, or light colours, whereas the designer produces colour by means of pigments. The red, yellow and blue of the spectrum can be reproduced only in "pure" form as pigments, i.e. they cannot be obtained by mixing any other pigments, thus are known as *primary* pigments. Every other colour can be produced by mixing two or more pigments together in varying amounts.

In the colour-circle, it will be observed that the lightest colour, yellow, appears opposite the darkest colour, indigo-blue, and the warm reds and oranges are situated opposite the cool blues and blue-greens. Colours directly opposite each other in the circle are known as complementary colours, and if used near together in a piece of work, they both react by appearing more vivid. Direct opposites, therefore, should be used in any colour scheme with great discretion, otherwise the effect may be unpleasantly garish.

A colour-scheme employing a combination of colours which appear opposite each other in the circle, is known as a "contrasting" colour-scheme. If properly used, it can give a lively and stimulating effect, otherwise it can easily produce one that is strident and jarring.

The chemist Michel Chevreul, a director of colour at the famous Gobelin tapestry works near Paris, summarised his *Laws of Colour Contrast*[1] as follows:

1. Whenever a dark colour is placed beside a light colour, the dark colour will appear darker and the light appear lighter.

2. Whenever a dull colour is placed beside a strong colour, the dull colour will appear duller, and the strong colour will appear stronger. Hues appear at greatest intensity when their complementaries are placed side by side.

3. Whenever a colour is placed beside another colour, such colour will tend towards the complementary of the other colour. For example, in a combination of red and blue, the red will tend towards orange, and will have a yellow-red cast, since red is the complementary

[1] *De la Loi du Contraste Simultané des Couleurs*, 1839.

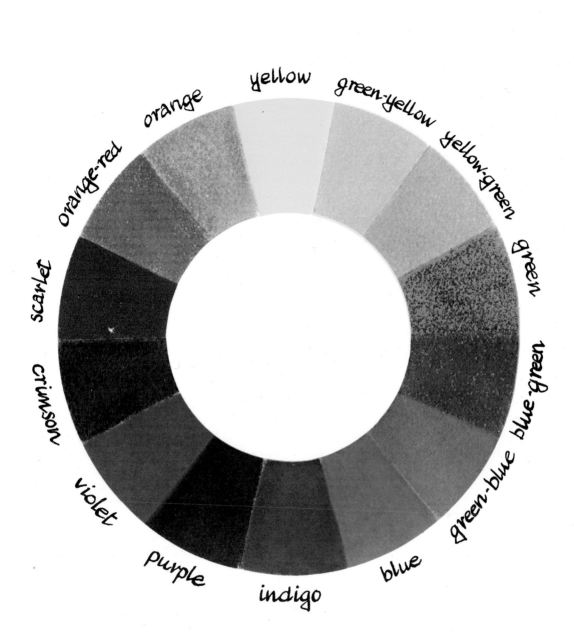

of blue. Blue, on the other hand, will tend towards blue-green, as blue-green is the true complementary of red.

A colour-scheme composed of a group of colours occurring near or adjacent to one another in the circle, will give a "harmonious" colour-scheme. If rightly composed, it produces a feeling of rest and satisfaction, but if not, it may become dull and boring. Any set of colours used in a colour-scheme, in which the same primary colour is an element, gives harmony by relation. A colour is sometimes deliberately introduced into an otherwise harmonious scheme, to which it is unrelated, in order to create a colour "discord", and if added in just the right proportion, can give valuable stimulus to the general scheme.

Every colour has its own true intensity, or *hue*, also an innumerable number of *shades*, obtained by adding varying amounts of black to the original hue, and *tints*, by similarly adding white. The degree of strength or intensity of a shade or tint is known as a *tone*, and a colour whose brightness has been damped down by the addition of grey tones, or of black, is a *neutral* colour.

Although the spectrum is composed of pure colours or hues, pure colours occur in nature relatively seldom, and there are infinitely more to be found that are greyed or neutral colours, or half-tones. The importance of having a good balance of tone-values in any colour scheme cannot be too strongly emphasised. Tones and half-tones used in the correct proportions give unity and balance to the design as a whole. Other factors are, of course, also significant, such as the colours themselves, surface textures, and the shapes composing the design, but without an appreciation of tone values, the total effect is bound to be diminished.

Simple tone variation

Trolley-cloth

Worked on the domestic sewing-machine. The cloth is bright yellow-green spun fabric, the embroidery in free running and darning-stitch in black, white, grey and pale pink.

Machine embroidery is a decorative medium in its own right, whose mode of expression is somewhere between graphic line drawing and the rich texture and pattern of hand embroidery. Here its fluent linear quality is well demonstrated. The needle is used like a pen, and the mechanical stitching produces a characteristic spiky and granular texture, which imparts a decorative quality to the work.

Designed and embroidered by ALISON LILEY.

Simple tone variation

A scheme using colours that all have the same tone-value will lack vitality, however pleasing the individual colours themselves may be, and, if pure hues are used, may become crude and gaudy. Bright colour is brought out and enhanced when in association with dull colour and half-tones. All colours react upon the eye in imparting to the beholder an impression of temperature, ranging from hot to cold. Warm or hot colours are exciting and stimulating, while cool or cold ones are restful, and a judicious balance of both is desirable. Warm colours are those containing substantial amounts of primary red, cool colours contain a high proportion of yellow, and cold colours are those occurring in the blue range. Generally speaking, individual preference for using one particular group of colours rather than another is based on personal temperament.

The embroiderer has her colours, tints and shades already prepared in many ranges of dyed threads, and in some respects is in a more advantageous position than workers in other media, who have to prepare their own. But this means she may be tempted to use too great a number of different colours in a piece of work, rather than few colours and more tones. The best way to develop an appreciation of tone-values is to work experimental motifs using light and dark contrasting tones of *one colour* only. It will be seen at once how pleasing and lively the effect can be. After a few disciplinary exercises of this nature, the worker may increase the number of colours she uses, but her experience should have taught her that it is the balance of tones that will give her design coherence and help to make it a unity. If we consider the monochromatic embroideries, such as traditional blackwork, whitework and counted-thread methods using self-colour, we see how the final effect depends not on pattern alone, but on the subtle variations of *tone* which the worker achieves by alterations in scale and spacing, and the relationship between worked, plain and open areas.

A tea-cosy

Worked on the domestic sewing-machine.

The material is white organdie and the design composed of decorative circular motifs derived from floral forms.

The embroidery is carried out in fine black lines, with coloured appliqué behind the centres of the motifs to produce a shadow effect. The scale and arrangement of the motifs have been carefully considered in relation to the size and shape of the cosy, in order to achieve a pleasing balance between the embroidered and plain areas.

Designed and embroidered by ENID MASON.

(*By courtesy of the Needlework Development Scheme*)

It is very important to understand that the true value of bright colour will not be brought out unless it is accompanied by subdued and neutral colour. The eye demands that a design shall be compounded of forms and colours which individually give opposing sensations of stimulus and repose, but collectively produce an effect of harmony. This is one of the reasons why the balance of shapes and tone-values in a design is essential. Colour is a complement of form, and must grow with the design, not be treated as something to be added extra. Bad colour can easily ruin an otherwise satisfactory design. The worker's choice of colour-scheme must be influenced by the ultimate purpose of the embroidery. Remember that flower embroidery is decoration, not portraiture, therefore it is not essential to use correct botanical colours; in fact the ornamental character of the design can be enhanced more effectively by the use of unnaturalistic colour. It is necessary to repeat once again that the essence of a flower lies not in its colour, but in certain qualities of form to which the colour is complementary.

. The worker should profit by studying the use of colour in textiles from the past, and in great paintings, but above all, she should keep her eyes open to the good use of colour *today*, in every aspect of contemporary living.

Six

FLOWER EMBROIDERY ON DRESS

"Brave flowers—that I could gallant it like you,
And be as little vain!"
Henry King, Bishop of Chichester, 1592–1669.

Iᴛ is perhaps appropriate to make a very general mention of floral embroidery used on historic costume. Our earliest existing examples in this country, which with one or two rare exceptions do not date from before the sixteenth century, were not sudden innovations of their own time, but take their place in a continuous sequence of dress decoration beginning well before the Norman Conquest.

Costume embroidery is naturally regulated by fashions in dress, which, in turn, are closely linked with social and political trends. An investigation of any particular period in dress cannot, therefore, omit a study of the latter if it is to be really understood. One must bear in mind, too, that embroidery on dress for everyday wear has always been the prerogative of the rich and nobly born, traditionally an indication of status, and thus concerning only a comparatively narrow section of the community.

Obviously very few textiles have survived from the ancient world, but in the pottery, sculptures, wall-paintings and writings of those times we possess a valuable record of the national dress and ornament of its civilisations. From descriptions left by the Romans of their first landing in Britain in 55 ʙ.ᴄ., it appears that the native dress consisted of coarse woollen or linen garments, generally woven in large, brightly coloured stripes or checks, with cloaks of animal skins. The inhabitants were divided up into a number of warring tribes and it seems improbable that embroidery figured among their arts.

The Romans occupied Britain for nearly four hundred years, during which time Britons living in or near the garrison towns became more or less Romanised, and high-ranking families came to wear the Roman form of dress. There is abundant evidence to show that Roman women were extremely skilful at embroidery, which had for centuries been an essential part of the dress of the Roman governing classes, and it is likely that the wives of the Occupation forces would have passed on many of their embroidery techniques to their British slaves. But the civilisation and order which the Romans brought to Britain did not remain for long after the Legions were recalled in A.D. 410. Their law, manners, and the Christian faith which they had introduced were utterly swept away by the Anglo-Saxon conquest, and their whole organisation of government and society disappeared as if it had never been. Over one hundred and fifty years passed before communications were once more established between Britain and the continent. The Roman Abbot, Augustine, landing with his monks in 597, brought back not only the Christian faith, but the civilisation, arts and letters which had fled before the invading Saxons. Though the country was to endure further centuries of war, revolution and change, it was following the return of Christianity to Britain, and its impact on the lives of the Saxon conquerors, that the foundations were laid of our great early tradition of English ecclesiastical embroidery.

But while the greatest skills and costliest materials were dedicated to embroidery for the church, a large amount was also worked for secular purposes outside the convents, in fact Anglo-Saxon women were renowned for their needlework. Saxon dress embroidery took the form of bright coloured borders around the neck, hem and sleeves of gowns, under-gowns and mantles, with later a centre panel from neck to hem, and an embroidered girdle. Male civilian dress was also bordered with embroidery at neck, sleeves and hem. Floral patterns were sometimes used, but the most popular motifs were circles, squares and dots, and the nobility favoured white tunics with gold embroidery, after the Byzantine manner. Costume styles and embroidered ornament underwent only slight changes for several centuries after the Norman Conquest. From the beginning of the eleventh century, England was ruled by a succession of foreign kings, under whom, notwithstanding, she developed her individualistic style of craftsmanship, which later was to flower into its finest expression during the thirteenth and early fourteenth centuries. Church sculptures, illuminated missals and MSS show that in essentials English costume changed very little from Anglo-Saxon times to the early fourteenth century, except for modifications in sleeve width or length of hem, but the bands of embroidery became deeper, and as the range of rich materials imported from the East grew, embroidery techniques became more elaborate, with jewels and appliqué.

The reigns of the first six Plantagenet Kings, with the exception of John, were notable for their restraint and simplicity, those of Edward I and Edward II, covering the period between 1272 to 1327, which produced the great church embroideries, or "Opus Anglicanum", being the least ostentatious of all. But following the accession of Edward III, a dramatic change in secular dress occurred. Tailoring was introduced for the first time, and the loose draperies which had been worn for centuries were now made to fit the figure.

An Elizabethan bodice
With floral embroidery arranged in the popular scrolling manner. Buttonhole fillings, hollie-point, French knots and seeding.
(*By courtesy of the Victoria & Albert Museum. Crown Copyright*)

As church embroidery declined in artistic refinement, embroidery on the costumes of the nobility became gorgeous and ornate. Every article of personal dress was richly ornamented with heraldic, geometric or floral designs. Sometimes these were printed or painted on to the material, and colours were always brilliant. Chaucer, describing the Squire, in his prologue to the *Canterbury Tales*, says:

> "Embrouded was he, as it were a meede
> Al ful of fresshe floures, whyte and reede."

At the beginning of the century, motifs were fairly small in scale, but as it wore on they became larger and larger, and occasionally enormous, and the fashion for counterchanged or parti-colours predominated. The national passion for extravagant display filled foreign visitors with wonder, and prompted Edward III to draw up sumptuary laws, aimed at restricting the heavy expenditure on fabrics, jewels and embroideries for personal adornment. These laws, re-enacted by successive monarchs, appear to have been singularly ineffective. In spite of crippling wars in which the country was involved throughout most of the fifteenth century, the Hundred Years War with France, succeeded by the Wars of the Roses, costumes became increasingly ornate. A few oil paintings appear for the first time in this century, and add to our records of contemporary dress.

During the Tudor period, attention began to be paid to the embroidering of undergarments. At first the visible portions of men's shirts were embroidered at the neck and wrists, usually with black silk and gold and silver thread, but later, embroidery was added to the fronts and sleeves also, and the outer garment slashed, so that these embroidered portions could be pulled through to show on the outside. There was a great development in skilled "fine" techniques, with cut-work and lace embroidery introduced as trimmings. The motifs by this time were predominantly floral, and diminished in scale as the century progressed. Portraits by Holbein and other painters show the exquisite effect of such intricate all-over patterning on rich plain fabric. Every part of the costume received embroidery, from ruff to shoes.

The reigning monarch in each period set the prevailing fashion in court dress, and the Tudor period was the most magnificent in our history. Masculine attire was even more gorgeous than feminine; and Elizabeth's three thousand dresses were equalled in their splendour by the velvets, ruffs and jewels of the courtiers round her, which gave rise to the saying that men "wore a manor on their backs".

From the middle of the sixteenth century we can date the rise of the conception of domestic comfort, which spread not only among the wealthy, but also among the middle classes and yeomanry. The prosperity resulting from expansion of foreign trade, and industry at home under Elizabeth, brought about marked changes in the home environment of all classes. Carpets instead of rushes on the floor, tapestry hangings and pillows, previously regarded as being fit only for women in child-bed, became necessary furnishings in the homes of the well-to-do. Our earliest surviving embroidered costumes and furnishings date from this time, and their survival may be due in part to the architectural improvements of Elizabeth's time—the attention paid to heating and ventilating, glazed windows, and furniture giving opportunities for better storage and preservation.

The English under the Tudors had a great love for flowers, and indeed for everything relating to nature and the countryside. Describing them, a Dutch visitor, coming to England in 1560, said:

"Their chambers and parlours strawed over with sweet herbes refreshed mee; their nosegays finely intermingled with sundry sorts of fragraunte floures, in their bed-chambers and privy-rooms, with comfortable smell cheered mee up, and entirely delyghted all my senses . . ."

The general interest in plants and especially garden flowers, which grew up in Elizabeth's reign, was fostered by the publication of quantities of herbals, which were originally "bookes of Physick" concerned with the illustrations of plants used for medicine, and which later developed into general histories of plants. Much contemporary floral needle-work was adapted from the wood-cut illustrations in these herbals, and the most popular flowers represented are familiar garden flowers of the period, the rose, carnation, daffodil or honeysuckle.

Tudor honeysuckle motif in
bullion and surface stitchery

Elizabethan scrolled honeysuckle

From Tudor times to the present, the costume of each successive period has been recorded for us by the principal painters of each era, and through them we obtain a complete picture of embroidery on dress for the past five hundred years. Some of the best floral work from the time of Charles I is undoubtedly to be found in needlemade lace. This particular medium seems to lend itself, above all, to the decorative treatment of flowers. Lace was made in England in Tudor times, although the best, finest and most costly came from abroad. The restricted technique of this method demanded a disciplined approach to design, which encouraged work of a high artistic standard. In mid-Victorian times, beautiful hand-made lace and hideous coloured flower embroidery were being produced at the same period.

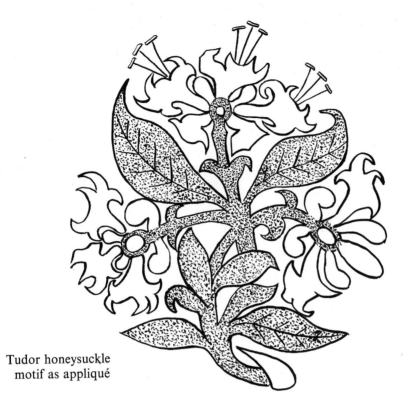

Tudor honeysuckle
motif as appliqué

The rapid increase in trade, especially with the East India Company in the mid-seventeenth century, accelerated the infiltration of foreign ideas into design, and encouraged rapid changes of fashion. The second half of the eighteenth century saw the introduction of flowered silk brocades from Spitalfields and abroad, resulting in a fall in demand for embroidery on dress, although embroidered waistcoats were worn throughout the Hanoverian period, and women's dresses were frequently ornamented with floral sprig patterns and appliqué. During the reign of Queen Anne, coloured flower embroideries were treated naturalistically, with elaborate shading after the oriental style introduced by chinoiserie, and it was sometimes combined with the most exquisite quilting, a type of embroidery which reached its zenith in this period.

The home production of flowered muslin for ladies' and children's wear, inspired by Indian imported cottons, led to the development of a particularly beautiful type of white floral embroidery, which was produced in Scotland in the early nineteenth century and known as Ayrshire work. Ayrshire embroidery was the outcome of a brief but happy partnership of art and commerce between the end of the Hanoverian and the Early Victorian era. As late as 1860 this exquisite work could still be found, when the depth of bad taste had been reached in other decorative art, and it proves, if nothing else does, that the separation of designer and craftsman need not be detrimental to good embroidery, but may, on the contrary, be a contributory factor to its success.

Early eighteenth-century apron: detail in shaded silks in the "chinoiserie" style.
(By courtesy of the Victoria & Albert Museum. Crown Copyright)

Flowered Hanoverian waistcoat

Probably between 1760–71. The ground is creamy satin, and the embroidery in peach, blue, brown and green silks, µsing flat-stitch, satin and encroaching satin, after the Chinese style.

This is the later, shorter type of waistcoat, sleeveless and with low hip pockets, which was worn buttoned up with the coat left open. The decoration is arranged so that it is displayed to best advantage.

(*By courtesy of the Needlework Development Scheme*)

Victorian white-work blouse-front
Fine lawn, with embroidered flowers in padded satin-stitch, eyelet holes and needle-lace fillings. An extremely charming and delicate design.
(*By courtesy of the Needlework Development Scheme*

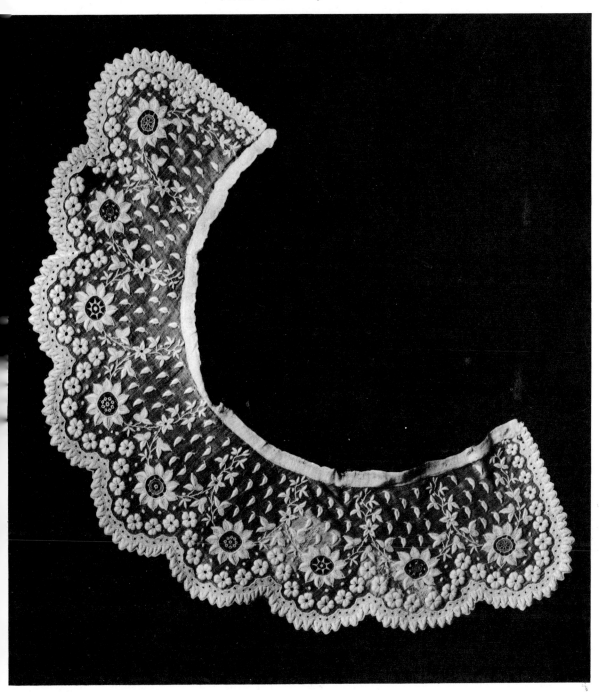

Victorian collar

Of fine lawn with scalloped edge and decoration of repeating floral motifs in white-work, using padded satin-stitch, trailing and various needle-lace fillings in the centres of the larger flowers.

(*By courtesy of the Needlework Development Scheme*)

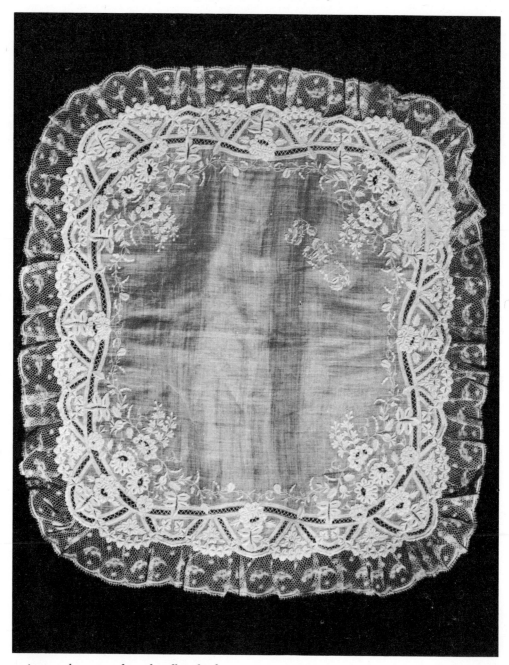

Late nineteenth-century lawn handkerchief
With fine white embroidery in the Ayrshire manner, including padded satin-stitch, trailing and lace openwork fillings.

The repeating border design is full of intricate detail, with a sensitive balance between linear and solid areas. It exemplifies the beautiful precision and elegance of this work.

(*By courtesy of the Needlework Development Scheme*)

The eventual decline of embroidery is attributed to the industrial revolution, but this is perhaps only part of the truth. The attitudes and values of any community dictate what kind of art it produces; we must take into account the changed status of women, and their subordinate role in society during the eighteenth and nineteenth centuries.

The restriction of women's lives, and trivialising of all things feminine, which began during the eighteenth century, was quite unknown in Tudor or Stuart times. Women living in these periods, and indeed before then, possessed a social freedom and responsibility for managing their everyday affairs, and shared life with their menfolk to a much greater degree than was permitted to their descendants. By the eighteenth century, trade expansion had led to a great increase in the wealth of the aristocratic and merchant classes, so that homes became more and more luxurious, family life sheltered, and a new social type emerged—the "lady of leisure".

Certain circumstances now arose which combined to have a fatal effect upon embroidery. From being a serious functional craft it diminished to an elegant diversion for the idle. But this was not all—male interest in embroidery had waned after it had gone out of fashion on gentlemen's dress at the beginning of the nineteenth century. It was considered an unmanly preoccupation, no longer a serious art, but an inferior relative of painting. Masculine collaboration was thus absent when sterner values were most needed, at a period notorious for its worship of bogus romanticism and sentiment.

The conception of embroidery as an apt medium for reflecting attitudes—for depicting whimsicality, "charm" or sentimentality, really stems from this time, and continues to exercise a strong influence today. It is this idea which has done much damage to the craft and its reputation. Sincerity and a measure of detachment in the statement of its theme are the necessary prerequisites of every piece of work, enabling the true individuality of the worker to reveal itself.

SHORT BIBLIOGRAPHY

Decorative Patterns of the Ancient World, Flinders Petrie, KT., F.R.S., F.B.A. (Bernard Quaritch Ltd, and London University Press.)

The Craftsman's Plant Book, Richard G. Hatton. (Chapman & Hall, 1909.)

Pattern and Design, N. I. Cannon. (Lund Humphries & Co., 1948.)

Design in Civilisation, Noel Carrington. (Bodley Head, 1947.)

The English Tradition in Design, John Gloag. (King Penguin Books, 1947.)

Traditional Methods of Pattern Designing, Archibald H. Christie. (Clarendon Press, Oxford, 1929.)

English Costume from the Second Century B.C. to 1952, Doreen Yarwood. (B. T. Batsford Ltd, 1952.)

The Flowerers, Margaret H. Swain. (W. & R. Chambers Ltd, 1955.)

The Paisley Shawl, Matthew Blair. (Alexander Gardner, 1904.)

The Costumes and Textiles of India, Jamila Brij Bhushan. (F. Lewis Ltd.)

DATE DUE

7 - '66

DE 1 '67

JA 3 '68

MY 10 68

JY15 70

NO 23 71

DE 5 72

FE 5 74

MR 476

AP 10 76

AP 26 76

FEB 24 77

JAN 2 8 1980

Fordham Equip. Co.

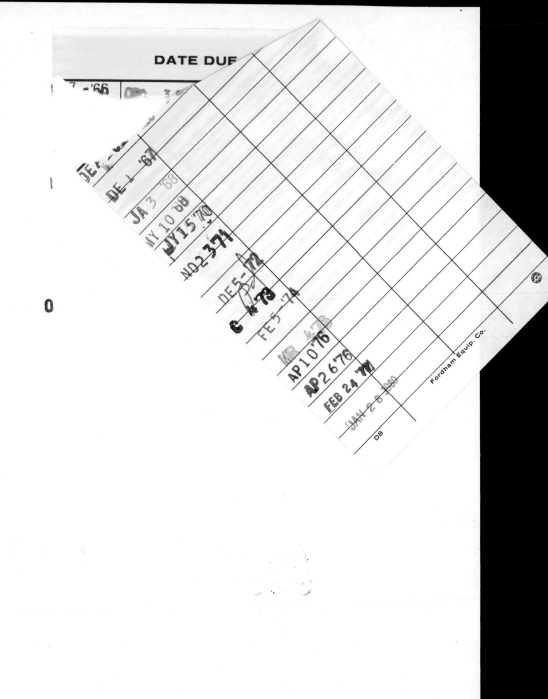